PLAYING THE GAME
OUR WAY

AMOS WHITTINGTON SR.

ISBN 979-8-88616-452-7 (paperback)
ISBN 979-8-88616-453-4 (digital)

Christian Faith Publishing
832 Park Avenue
Meadville, PA 16335
www.christianfaithpublishing.com

Printed in the United States of America

To my mother.
Even though we lost you over twenty-two years ago, your
memory lives on in me. I can still hear you tell me to start over
and do it better the next time. I do that with everything.
I love you, Mom, Ms. Annie L. Whittington. RIP.

CHAPTER 1

The Speech

It didn't hit me until the morning of that I had been chosen to do the commencement speech for my elementary school's class graduation. It wasn't that I was nervous. I just couldn't believe that my teacher chose me to do such an important thing. You see, I had been known as the class clown throughout elementary school. But this was my chance to grow up. I remember writing the speech over and over and over again until, finally, my mother insisted that it was good. After my classmates voted, and I was told that my essay was chosen, I felt a sense of relief and a sense of honor.

My morning started off with the smell of bacon and oatmeal, my favorite. My brother Harvey had already left to catch his bus to his school. My brother was a year older, and he was already in the same school that I was set to go to. I did feel some comfort that my brother would be around, just in case I needed his help. After all, the school that I was set to attend had a reputation of being a little rough. As my mother and I waited for my aunt and uncle to come pick us up for graduation, I went over my notes and reflected on this new adventure that I was about to step into. I just remembered being known as a little kid, and now I'm a big boy, I thought to myself. During the speech, I remembered my teacher telling me that if I get nervous, just focus on one or two people in the audience. So I followed his advice and zeroed in on a girl that I liked named Chanel.

It must've worked because I got a standing ovation and a kiss on the cheek from Chanel. It was hard for me to believe that once I left that school that day, I would never return.

CHAPTER 2

Summer Vacation

EVERY SUMMER, MY family in Maryland would venture down South to the great state of North Carolina. It seemed like my entire family lived in North Carolina, except us of course. I enjoyed the long ride and the old classic music my grandfather would play. This was in the late '70s, early '80s, and life seemed to be so simple then. This was Labor Day weekend. The roads were packed with other families headed South. Quite often, my grandfather would stop on the side of the road to various restaurants and gas stations. I always enjoyed stopping because he would always get snacks. My grandmother, on the other hand, hated stopping because she wanted to get on down the road. It seemed like it would always be nighttime when we left Baltimore and nighttime when we would arrive in North Carolina. As an adult driver now, the ride doesn't seem as long. I believe my grandfather was taking the scenic route. Every year, it seemed like our family down South was steadily expanding. Cousins that I didn't even know I had would walk up to me and say, "Hey, cuz."

I was always told that there's nothing like Southern hospitality. Whoever said that was so right. I felt like I never wanted to leave whenever it was time to go. All the good cooking, the smell of fresh air, and did I mention my Aunt Rossy's good cooking? My mother was born and raised in North Carolina, my brother was born in Baltimore, and I was born in North Carolina as well. No matter where we chose to call home, North Carolina will and has always been our home.

Labor Day weekend was always a long weekend, but for some reason, this particular Labor Day weekend was short. Maybe because I was nervous about junior high school. At any rate, I tried to focus on having fun with my family. We had various events at the reunion. But no event meant more to me than the annual softball game. I always believed that I was a gifted athlete, and it was my time to show my family just how special I was. I remember that day like it was yesterday. In my mind, I had a career day. Three homers, three stolen bases, in my defense at short stop was worthy of a golden glove. I was probably the only one keeping score that day. My brother, Harvey, was pretty good that day too. Mostly all of my cousins were girls, but we all had game.

It was the last play of the game, and it was something that only happened in movies. You know? The bottom of the ninth inning, three balls, two strikes. I was up, and I had the chance to be legendary. Before I knew it, I had hit the ball into deep left field where one of my cousins had struggled at all day. But this time, she was able to field the ball with no trouble. As I rounded third, headed for home plate, I could see my brother standing on home plate, waiting for the ball to arrive! Suddenly, as I started to dive head first, my left shoulder collided into my brother's leg, and everything went blank! Just like that, I had broken my collarbone. I remember the pain being so excruciating that all I could do was cry!

The next morning, we all woke up early to begin the long journey home. Everyone in the car seemed to be in a pretty good mood, except for me. I knew that starting a new school year at a new school would be hard enough. Now I had to start it with an injury. What would these older students think of me? What kind of mean and nasty words would they call me? Oh well, at least my mother assured me that I wouldn't have to report to school until after I had seen a doctor. As we inched closer and closer back home, I wondered if my grandpa would stop for a bathroom break. Lo and behold, my grandma said she needed to use the restroom. This seemed to never happen! My grandma always talked about not liking to use, what she called, filthy public bathrooms. How rare was this? So we all piled out of the car and into the travel plaza gas station. Suddenly it dawned on me that I was struggling to undress to use the bathroom. Okay, it wasn't like I was getting naked or something, just simply unbuttoning my pants. I was thirteen years old and embarrassed because my brother had to help me unzip my pants. I have to admit, I was still in pain. After that embarrassing moment, my grandpa asked me if a gift from the gift shop would make me feel better. Of course, I said, "Yes." I picked up several things, but only one thing I could get. So I chose a ring! Sterling silver ring with the head of a wolf attached! *Pretty cool!* I thought.

"Do not wear that ring to school, Amos!" my mother said.

I was thinking to myself, *Yeah, right, Mother dear. I must show this ring off!*

As the night grew closer, so did the city of Baltimore! We were finally back home. The sounds of sirens and people said home. I was beginning to miss down South already.

CHAPTER 3

The First Day

ONE WEEK AFTER my accident, I was all set to start school. We had just returned home from church that Sunday when my best friend, James, came to visit me. He was shocked that my arm was in a sling. "What happened to you?" he said.

I responded by telling him about the softball game and that my collarbone was broken. The look on his face was priceless. "So how are you going to fight tomorrow?" he said.

I said, "Well, I don't intend to fight anyone!" I asked him what he had gotten himself into and why I was supposed to fight.

He began to tell me about a bully that had been picking on him since last week. None of this really surprised me. James had always been picked on. But the thing about him was that he always picked fights with people bigger than him. He never backed down from anything. That's why this situation was a bit unusual. I was thinking that the guy he needed me to fight must be way bigger than both of us. We talked a little while longer, and before we knew it, my mother was calling me in the house for dinner. The whole time at the dinner table, all I could think about was, *How am I supposed to fight someone with a broken collarbone?*

The very next day came faster than I wanted it to. My mom could always tell that something was wrong with me, but that morning, I tried to put on an act to throw her off. Needless to say, before

I gave her a hug goodbye, she said, "Be safe, and don't get into any trouble behind that crazy little boy." My mom liked James, but she could always figure out my friends. "Did you put on any deodorant, boy?" my mom asked me.

"Um, yes," I said. It was half true because of my left shoulder still being sore.

A group of my friends came to my house to pick me up so that we could walk to school together. The school was about three miles from my house. I couldn't imagine walking that far nowadays. We walked through neighborhoods that had abandoned houses, cars, and drug paraphernalia on the ground. Most of the people we encountered on the way to school told us to have a good day and to learn something. When we finally arrived, I noticed that there were White students as well as Black. I was a bit excited about having another race in my class. Most of the White students were bused in from various neighborhoods. I must admit that they looked a little scared while they sat on their bus. Some of the Black students mocked them and threw eggs at the buses. I didn't see the need to join in. I was raised better than that.

As we walked toward the front of the school, we saw about three different fights going on. This to me was not what I imagined this school would be like. But my brother warned me that it was crazy sometimes. My friends left me at the main office so that I could find out where my homeroom class was. The principal met me in the lobby and welcomed me to hell. I proceeded to walk to my new classroom down this long hallway. As I began to walk toward my classroom, the principal called me back and asked me about the ring I had on my finger. I explained to him that it was a gift from my grandpa. He informed me that I couldn't have that type of ring on while in the building. He said that it could be considered a weapon because of how it's made. So he confiscated it until the end of the school day. I didn't think anything of it.

As I entered the class, I noticed that I knew a few students from my neighborhood. That made me feel a little better about the class. The teacher seemed to have little or no control over the class. She simply told me to find an empty desk and be seated. When the class finally settled down a bit, I was introduced to everyone by my teacher Mrs. Smith. It was very awkward standing there while everyone was looking at me, trying to figure me out. Throughout the day, I had to introduce myself to every class I entered. I could not wait until this day was over. It was pretty warm that day. I was starting to sweat, and I remember not being able to put deodorant under my left armpit.

Suddenly someone said that they smelled onions. I knew it was me smelling like that. My teacher asked if anyone needed deodorant. I surprised myself by standing up and admitting that I was the one who was smelling. I believed that day, while being embarrassed, I earned respect from my teacher and classmates just by being honest.

As the end of the day drew closer, I was reminded by James that I still had to fight. I didn't even know who the person was I was supposed to fight, until suddenly, the guy walked up and said to me, "If you think faking like your arm hurts is going to stop me from beating you down, you're wrong." This guy seemed to be very confident in himself. It wasn't that I was scared, I just didn't understand why I had to fight him. But he was bigger than James, and I had always taken up for him. But something had to give. I couldn't keep fighting other people's battles.

As the bell rang to announce the end of the day, people began to whisper about all the fights, including mine. I walked to the principal's office and got my ring back from him. As soon as I stepped out of the front door, the guy was standing there, waiting for me. My brother, Harvey, James, and a bunch of other kids stood waiting to see this fight. I thought maybe my brother would jump in between and demand that I don't. Not a chance. Harvey looked at me and said, "Get him."

So we started sizing each other up. At this moment, I had released my arm from the sling and began to punch back. Before I knew it, this guy had thrown me to the ground. The crowd screamed, "Get him! Kick him!"

I didn't know if they were on my side or not. When I realized that I was losing the fight, I remembered that ring I had on my finger. So I did the unthinkable. I hit this guy in the center of his head with my fist. He screamed while blood poured from his head. The fight was over. He ran away, and I got hauled off to the principal. I got suspended from school for one week. My mom wasn't exactly upset, and she wasn't happy either. Nevertheless, I won the fight.

CHAPTER 4

The Unthinkable

WITH THE FIGHT and my suspension in the past, the first quarter of my first year at Harlem Park was underway. I settled in pretty quickly with my classmates. We had several issues that resulted in fighting and yelling amongst students. Sometimes, we would witness kids fighting teachers. The real battle was just getting to school safely. Outside of school was a whole different experience. The neighborhood that was called Sand Town challenged everyone who lived there. Police officers were visible on every corner, it seemed, but that didn't seem to bother the neighborhood drug dealer. Countless drug overdoses were an everyday event. People who lived on my block would warn me about the threat of being a statistic. I didn't quite understand what they meant until I witnessed kids my age adapt to the stress and struggle of the mean streets of Baltimore. People who I often played basketball and football with were suddenly drug dealers. They would show off the latest shoes and clothes. Some even had cars. It didn't impress me at all. Even though we were poor, my family had dreams of becoming successful, opening up businesses, and buying real estate. Even at twelve, I dreamed big and beyond my years.

Reality hit me one day after school. As we walked toward my house, I could see furniture and other things that belonged to me out in front of my house. My mother sat, crying because we had been evicted. I didn't want to seem upset or cause my mom anymore heartache, so I simply gave her a hug. But my mom, being the strong woman that she was, pushed me away and said, "Let's take what we can around the corner to my friend's house until I can figure everything out." Before we knew it, things were back to normal. My grandma came to the rescue, and we were able to move into another house. The worse part about everything to me was watching my mom struggle to find work. Without skills and a degree, finding a good-paying job was enough to drive a sane person insane. But eventually work came, and Mom enjoyed her job. She worked a lot of late nights. That would mean she wouldn't be home by the time we got in. So I became the cook, and I also would help Harvey with his homework as well as my own.

One day while in school, a bell rang during the middle of one of my classes. This was pretty unusual. Following the bell, a voice repeated over and over that there should not be any students in the hallways and for teachers to lock their classroom doors. No one said a word. Even our teacher had a look of concern on her face. Finally, after an hour of waiting, we all got news that a student had been shot inside of the school. We were all dismissed and sent home for the remainder of the day.

When I got home from school, I watched the news and learned that the student died from his injuries. I didn't know the student personally, but ironically, his younger brother was in one of my classes. Later on that evening, Mom called to check on us. She asked if I wanted transfer to another school. I thought about it a while, and eventually, I decided to stay. The school seemed different and calm since the shooting. Kids were told to walk in groups, in and around the school. We learned later on that the motive for the shooting was over a jacket.

As days and weeks went by, the notion that could have been me or my brother stuck in my head. The emotional roller coaster that the tragedy brought in and around our school was apparently affecting what people thought of the neighborhood and school. Parents began to transfer their kids out, teachers left for other opportunities. The buses that once dropped off White kids to our school suddenly didn't exist. There were only a few White kids left in our school. The shame of it all was that a family was left without a loved one, a young man who I learned was a great basketball player and a wonderful son and brother. The loss of a loved one is never easy to accept, especially when someone takes them away from you. I looked for other things to do in school to keep a positive attitude.

I remember walking pass the music room, and I heard the song "We Are the World" being sung. I walked inside and began singing. The music teacher asked me where I belonged. I told the teacher that I was in Spanish class and that I was just walking by. I was told by the teacher that I had to sign up for the class. Eventually I did and ended up joining the school choir, just to have something to do. There I met other students from other classes that I would see but would never talk to. I enjoyed attending rehearsals. I always thought that I had a nice voice. It showed when I got to sing one of the lead vocals. The song, "We Are the World," was fitting and somewhat amazing. For our school to have gone through such a tragedy, the song was on time. Our city needed healing. No government or state official could do it. "We Are the World" stood for something more than just a great song. It stood for a time of healing and time to love and cherish what God has brought us through.

CHAPTER 5

The Wintertime Blues

THE THREAT OF snow gloomed over the city of Baltimore all winter. But not even the snow could stop the violence that plagued our great city. I remember my relatives down South, wishing that they could live in the city like us. But for me, it was just the opposite. I always wanted to get away and live somewhere warmer and safer. The cold weather didn't seem to bother the drug dealers or addicts. They still lined the corners and alleyways, making their deals. Kids like myself saw this as a normal everyday theme. The drug dealers I knew always had the latest sneakers and sweatsuits and jewelry on. That alone would make a young man like myself want to follow their lead. But most of the dealers would warn us of the dangerous lifestyles and would tell us to stay in school and go to college. Some of the addicts were people I knew from the block that seemed ashamed when I would see them in the dope lines. Nevertheless, I would never disrespect them or their lifestyle. After all, I had family members that got high.

The wintertime wasn't all that cold that year. I met a young lady who lived only blocks away from me who went to my school. Her name was Trish. We ended up walking to school together in the snow every once in a while. Eventually she became my girlfriend. We weren't sexually active or nothing. Holding hands was all right by me. Of course, that didn't sit well with the rest of my friends. I didn't care. Trish would compliment me on the way I dressed and my mannerism. I owed it all to my Aunt Linda who always taught me that I should be kind to people, if I wanted people to be kind to me. Throughout the rest of the school year, I began to mature and get out of my comfort zone. Eventually Trish and I became distant friends but always called each other best friends.

My collarbone healed up, and I was able to play pickup basketball at the neighborhood recreation center. I wasn't the best basketball player by far, but I would hold my own. Baltimore City has always been known, for years, as a city that breeds great ball players. Sports, for years, has saved the lives of many inner-city kids. It was a ticket out of the streets. I can remember playing basketball from sun up to sun down. Even the neighbors wouldn't complain about the noise we would make while playing. Some police officers would come out and play a game or two. Now people don't seem to trust cops like we did.

Before I knew it, I was moving on to eighth grade. Life in the city didn't change any. Crime was still visible from block to block. My mother moved us to another house not too far from the same area we'd lived most of my life. The best part about this neighborhood to me was that we lived one block from a playground that had its own basketball courts. I grew taller over the summer, but I was still considered short to most of my friends. At five feet, nine inches, I played and acted like I was seven feet tall, never showed any fear, even if I was afraid. The hood taught us that.

My new neighbors were nice to us. People seemed to help one another through hard times. The struggle was real, but when you grow up poor, you can't seem to tell the difference. Food stamps helped with groceries, and the welfare system helped us pay the rent. So there was nothing left to do but pray. My mom still worked a part-time job to get us school clothes and miscellaneous stuff that helped us feel normal.

I started seeing a change in my brother. He started hanging out late at night and missing school. Eventually he got in trouble with the law. My mom couldn't control his actions and tried to provide a roof for us at the same time. Back and forth he went through the system. "Institutions, jail, or death is where you're headed," my mom would preach. But nothing seemed to change with my brother. I would pray at night that God would just bring him home safe. Eventually Harvey's actions would become a normal thing to me. I surrounded myself around my family and close friends.

In the '80s, west Baltimore, at times, was a dangerous place to live. Even now in 2020, nothing has really changed. I guess it's all a part of city life. Summers in the city meant Maryland blue crabs. Crabs and Baltimore went together like salt and pepper. We managed to turn some difficult and trying times into good times and everlasting moments. As bad as things seemed in the city, crabs always seemed to make things better. I spent summers fishing on my grandfather's boat and crabbing down on the eastern shore with my aunt Corine. My aunt Corine was one of my mom's closest sisters. She allowed me to come and stay with her for a summer, and I was able to work in Ocean City, Maryland. I even bought my own school clothes that year. That really helped my mom. Family has always been very important in my community.

CHAPTER 6

Back to the Books

DURING MY FIRST year in junior high, I did enough to pass on to the eighth grade. I was not on the honor roll, and my grades were just average. That didn't satisfy my mom. So I had to do something different this year, I thought to myself. I started asking for extra-credit assignments and staying after school for coach classes. Eventually my grades started to improve. The self-proclaimed class clown was now leaning toward being an A student. I started focusing on making the leap from junior high to high school almost immediately. I had less than a year to figure out what kind of changes I had to make to have a smooth transition to being a better student.

One day, out of the blue, an announcement came over the loud-speaker in school about any students wanting to participate in sports. We were told to meet in the gymnasium after school for further details. I was extremely excited about the opportunity play any sport. Just about all of my friends showed up to see what the announcement was about. Our gym teacher Coach Earl Banks presented us with an opportunity to play lacrosse. We all had never really heard of lacrosse until that day. Coach Banks gave us a brief history lesson on Black players such as the legendary Jim Brown who excelled in the sport. I only knew of Jim Brown being a professional football player, not a lacrosse player. To me, this was a White sport. Coach Banks held a lacrosse stick in hand, along with a weird-looking ball that was different in weight than a baseball but the same shape. The lacrosse sticks had a net on the end of it were the ball set. He threw the ball from the net up against the wall and caught it with the stick. We were amazed at how simple it appeared, but when we were given the opportunity to perform the same exercise, it didn't turn out the same as when Coach Banks did it. The ball bounced awkwardly as it returned from hitting the wall. Some students decided that lacrosse was not for them and decided to leave. There were only a few students who stayed for the demonstration. I was always up to any sport-related challenge, so I stayed as well. At the end of the session, we had to take home a permission slip to have our parents sign it. This was a very exciting and inviting time for us, especially after a heartbreaking and disappointing first year.

The next several weeks involved a two-hour practice that didn't go so well. Several students weren't able to participate because of their grades. Now just imagine how good I felt that my grades allowed me to participate. It was an amazing time in and around our school. Even the people who lived in the neighborhood by our school were excited. Our coach allowed us to carry our lacrosse sticks home to practice in our leisure. People would ask us about the lacrosse sticks. "Where are you going? Fishing?" The sport was definitely different from basketball, baseball, and football. Those were the only sports we had ever played in our neighborhood. We even had two girls who came out for the team.

I had a normal routine after school. I had to do my homework, help my brother with his, and cook dinner. The reason was that my mother had to work at night. Now that I had joined the lacrosse team, things were different and more challenging. Needless to say, I worked it out.

Several of my teammates caught on to using the lacrosse stick better than others. I struggled quite a bit. I was used to running with a football in my arms or basketball in my hand. This sport was different. It actually took more precise thinking than I was used to. But I stayed with it. After a while, the team started to improve their performance at practice and in classrooms. We got closer. Our first scrimmage took place at Forest Park High School, against the high school lacrosse team. We ended up losing the game but was given a sign of approval from the opposing coach. He told us that we played good enough to win the game but needed to practice more. The interesting thing about this team was that we were the only African American team in the league that we were to participate in.

The other schools were predominately White and had been playing the sport for years. This may have seemed to others as an unfair advantage, but for us, it was just another challenge. Being involved in this new sport took us away from whatever was going on in the hood, even if it was just for a while.

Things were pretty much the same in my neighborhood. Some of the people who I grew up with started disappearing. Some were arrested for various crimes, and some had been killed. Some moved out to other neighborhoods. But some of us had no other choice but to stay. We made the best of our situation just by being kind to our neighbors and looking forward to better days. I don't think, if I had the chance, that I would change the way I grew up. West Baltimore taught me to be the man I am today. Through the good times and bad times, we survived.

I remember the first official game on our schedule. We played against a team from Loyola Middle School. We had hosted the game, and the neighborhood showed up to support us. The Harlem Park Bulldogs was our name. There were signs all over the school and the neighborhood that said, "This Is Bulldog Country." We ended up losing our first few games of the season, but we were determined to improve. And we did. Whether it was playing at home or away, we made our opponents fear the Bulldogs. There were several talks about teams being afraid to come to our school to play because it was in the hood. So I guess that was a big advantage for us. Nevertheless, our play on the field showed what we were made of. Win after win, we grew closer to being the best team in the league. We were bigger and stronger than any opponent we faced. The skill set from the other teams showed as well. Game after game, there were challenges. Sometimes, we had to play shorthanded because of suspension or bad grades. But we showed up. I remember traveling to play at other schools and hearing racial slurs. This was very new to some of us.

After all, this was not the '50s and '60s! This was 1985. Things were supposed to be different. We were just kids trying to enjoy this new adventure. Just like anything else, we ignored the noise and kicked butt!

As the season went on, we were notified by our coach that we would be in the playoffs. What an accomplishment from a team put together in weeks with no experience. Our head coach was assisted by a coach named Mr. Shaw who was an English teacher with no coaching experience. Crazy, right? So we started preparing for the playoffs for the next several weeks. I played the position of midfield. This position required lots of running. So in my spare time, I would run around the city. Some areas that I would venture into were not too inviting. But, nevertheless, I was on a mission. My teammates in every position depended on me. Respect and responsibility was what I was looking for.

The physical nature of the game took a toll on the females that played with us. But that didn't stop one who continued to battle alongside of us each week. As a team, we won and lost together, but we stayed team strong.

As the word got around that we would be going to the playoffs, our celebrity-like status grew. The news reporters would show up at our practices. It was mostly about the other team and how they felt about playing an all-Black lacrosse team in the hood. Yet we stayed focused. The game was probably never meant to be played as physical as we played but that was our way. Fast and strong!

Leaving school and returning home every day was always in the back of my mind. Not knowing what the situation was, lacrosse seemed to take me away from all of the negative things that I would face at home. Lacrosse also enlightened me on the possibilities of changing a negative situation into a positive one. Family was always an encouraging factor for me. Having my family around to witness what we saw as historical was priceless.

CHAPTER 7

Reality

No matter how successful we became, that didn't stop my acne. These were teenage things that were out of my control. But being the celebrity I thought I was, people, especially girls, didn't mind. I never saw myself as a ladies' man. I was too much of a class clown. My mother spent so much money on acne medication that it was pathetic. I was certainly not the only kid in school with an acne problem. It just seemed like mine was just completely out of control.

As the playoffs gradually drew near, we practiced, what seemed like, night and day. Brushing up on our skills and running drill after. It was clear to me that we had turned into a really good team. We had earned the respect from all teams and our community. Sometimes, our own community wouldn't support our cause and dreams. So it was important to us that we had to be winners. Bringing home a championship trophy would be an incredible win for our community. A trophy was not going to stop the senseless killings or police brutality, but it could provide hope to the next generation of student athletes to attend Harlem Park.

As the playoffs got underway, we were notified by our coach that several of our teammates had gotten suspended from school. This was nothing new for us. Fighting and neighborhood altercations would always seem to show up when you least expect it. But this didn't stop Coach Banks from rearranging the lineup. The first and second team had to be split up into one team. We had such a large team that there was never really a time when one player had to play the entire game without rest. Yet, as soon as the playoffs started, we were in unfamiliar territory. Roddy and Bobby had to play more minutes than any of us. Not only were they the best one-two combinations on our team, they were probably the best in the league. Even though teams knew who they were, they couldn't stop them. We dominated our first ever playoff game with an impressive win over Loyola. Loyola had no answer for our fast and physical play. At one point, their coaches complained to the refs that we were trying to hurt their players. I can honestly say that in some cases, we were.

At the end of the game, we learned from our coaches that we were going to host the championship game. What a time this was. No one thought that this was possible. A group of misfits was what one reporter described us as. We even doubted ourselves in the beginning. Why wouldn't we? After all, this was a new game to us. It wasn't football, baseball, or basketball. This was lacrosse!

By the time I got home from the game, my entire neighborhood knew what we had accomplished. Remembering the doubts and the negative comments from people didn't stop me from smiling back at people who wished us well. My mother attended the game that day, but she had to leave early for work. I couldn't wait to tell her about the outcome. My brother, Harvey, had recently gotten into trouble, so he was not around. I went into the house to find that my mom had left a note on the fridge. She always left notes on what to do once we got home. Since Harvey wasn't home, the note was for me. Taped to the note was a five-dollar bill. The note read: "Congratulations on the win. I love you and go get you something from Burger King." This was such a surprise because my mother hardly ever allowed us to eat fast food. One reason was because we didn't really have the money, most of the time. And, also, because Burger King was in a not-so-good area to go. I decided not to go to Burger King. Instead, I kept the money for a rainy day.

Two weeks went past, and we were a few days from the championship. There was a buzz around the school like I've never seen. Kids who didn't seem to care about the game of lacrosse we're talking about joining the team the next season. For most of the team, it would be one and done. I was looking ahead to my future and wondering, *Would my high school have a lacrosse team or would this be it? Would I ever play again or even be interested in playing on the high school level? Maybe or maybe not.* This experience was unbelievable and full of ups and downs. I learned a new game, and I learned that racism was alive and well. Most of the teams we played were probably unaware of the names we were being called during the season. It didn't bother me much, especially while were winning. No matter what, our coaches kept most of the negativity away from us.

Game day was finally here. The field was painted with our Bulldog mascot and our green and white colors everywhere. We wore brand-new uniforms provided by several local sponsors. If anything, we looked good. The game didn't start off so well as we found our-selves down by two points. We ended up going into halftime, down by one point. During the halftime speech from our coaches, we were reminded that we didn't come this far to lose. Our opponent was Friends School. Friends were the defending champions of the league. During the season, we were able to beat them on their own field. On this day, they played just as physical as we did. Up and down the field we went during the second half. I hadn't scored a goal in a couple of games. The goalie they had was stopping everything that came near him. I had a few attempts earlier in the first half. I noticed that they would double-team our main scores. This left me and Greg to try and steal a few shots.

One after the other, Greg and I fired off several attempts at this goalie, and finally, we broke through. My goal tied up the game, and Greg's gave us the lead. Once we had the lead, there was no turning back. We could hear the crowd as they would rock the stands, cheer-ing so loud that when Friends had the ball, they couldn't communi-cate with each other. As the final whistle blew, the crowd rushed the field to congratulate us. We were champions. The impossible was now the possible. People who doubted us were now believers. The bullies even respected us. There wasn't a big game check to receive or a diamond ring to wear. Not even a parade. But respect and honor were evident.

I'm often reminded of the fun we had as a team. Even as an adult, I find myself picking up a lacrosse stick and pretending to score the game-winning goal. I also remind myself of the lives lost during that season. No, I'm not known as a legend or ever the best on the team, but I was a student athlete that learned how to play a new game that helped shape me into the man I am today. We all take steps to become the best we can be. I am now a grandfather and a father of three. The lessons I learned back in those days still help shape me. Not a lot has changed in the great city of Baltimore. Crime is still a major issue for city hall, and the educational system still has challenges. I still take trips to North Carolina with my family, but things have changed. I now drive like my grandfather used to. My mother passed a few years ago, and my brother and I are now the heads of our own families. The memories of playing lacrosse and fighting pimples still linger in my head. How great and exciting those days were. Even the bad times that give me chills, yay, they also remind me of how far I've come. The lacrosse field where I used to play is now empty, and the neighborhood is mostly boarded up. But if you listen closely, I swear, you can hear the crowd screaming, "This is bulldog country!"

ABOUT THE AUTHOR

AMOS WHITTINGTON SR.—THE father, the husband, and grandfather—has had a heck of a ride. The life of a little Black kid growing up in the city of Baltimore, he had to learn a lot on his own. Growing up poor and poverty stricken in the '70s had its fun times and really bad times. He often dreamed of being rich and famous, only to wake up to a dark place where nobody could save him, not even his hero, his mother. His mother struggled with alcohol abuse and abusive relationships. Still she raised two sons in the jungle that they called home. He saw it all. School was a place he could release the stress of just everyday life. Even while going through tough times, he found comfort in sports. Sports generally offered a few hours of peace, peace that seemed perfect at times. Coaches became fathers to the fatherless and mothers to the motherless. Today, as a father, grandfather, and husband, Amos takes the time to mentor and love without being asked. Even though his wife didn't know the athlete or child he was, she often sees glimpses of who he was as an athlete and child. Still competitive as ever, he pushes on and leads by example. This book has only a period of time that stands out a little more than other times. I'm sure that there's more from him to come.